CELEBRATING HOLIDAYS

Independence Day

by Rachel Grack

BELLWETHER MEDIA • MINNEAPOLIS, MN

Note to Librarians, Teachers, and Parents:

Blastoff! Readers are carefully developed by literacy experts and combine standards-based content with developmentally appropriate text.

Level 1 provides the most support through repetition of high-frequency words, light text, predictable sentence patterns, and strong visual support.

Level 2 offers early readers a bit more challenge through varied simple sentences, increased text load, and less repetition of high-frequency words.

Level 3 advances early-fluent readers toward fluency through increased text and concept load, less reliance on visuals, longer sentences, and more literary language.

Level 4 builds reading stamina by providing more text per page, increased use of punctuation, greater variation in sentence patterns, and increasingly challenging vocabulary.

Level 5 encourages children to move from "learning to read" to "reading to learn" by providing even more text, varied writing styles, and less familiar topics.

Whichever book is right for your reader, Blastoff! Readers are the perfect books to build confidence and encourage a love of reading that will last a lifetime!

This edition first published in 2018 by Bellwether Media, Inc.

No part of this publication may be reproduced in whole or in part without written permission of the publisher. For information regarding permission, write to Bellwether Media, Inc., Attention: Permissions Department, 5357 Penn Avenue South, Minneapolis, MN 55419.

Library of Congress Cataloging-in-Publication Data

Names: Koestler-Grack, Rachel A., 1973- author.
Title: Independence Day / by Rachel Grack.
Description: Minneapolis, MN : Bellwether Media, Inc., 2018. | Series: Blastoff! Readers: Celebrating Holidays | Includes bibliographical references and index. | Audience: Grades K-3. | Audience: Ages 5-8.
Identifiers: LCCN 2016052729 (print) | LCCN 2016054064 (ebook) | ISBN 9781626176225 (hardcover : alk. paper) | ISBN 9781681033525 (ebook)
Subjects: LCSH: Fourth of July–Juvenile literature. | Fourth of July celebrations–Juvenile literature.
Classification: LCC E286 .A1384 2018 (print) | LCG E286 (ebook) | DDC 394.2634–dc23
LC record available at https://lccn.loc.gov/2016052729

Editor: Christina Leighton • Designer: Lois Stanfield
Printed in the United States of America, North Mankato, MN.

Table of Contents

Independence Day Is Here!

American flags wave from flagpoles. People are wearing red, white, and blue.

pinwheel

Children play with colorful **pinwheels**. Happy Independence Day!

What Is Independence Day?

Independence Day is also called the Fourth of July.

Americans honor the United States on this day. They celebrate their freedom.

People across the United States enjoy Independence Day.

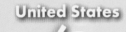

United States

It is a **national** holiday.
Many businesses close so
people can celebrate.

Independence Day Beginnings

George Washington

American **colonies** were once ruled by Great Britain. **Colonists** were unhappy with British rule.

In 1775, they began the **American Revolutionary War**.

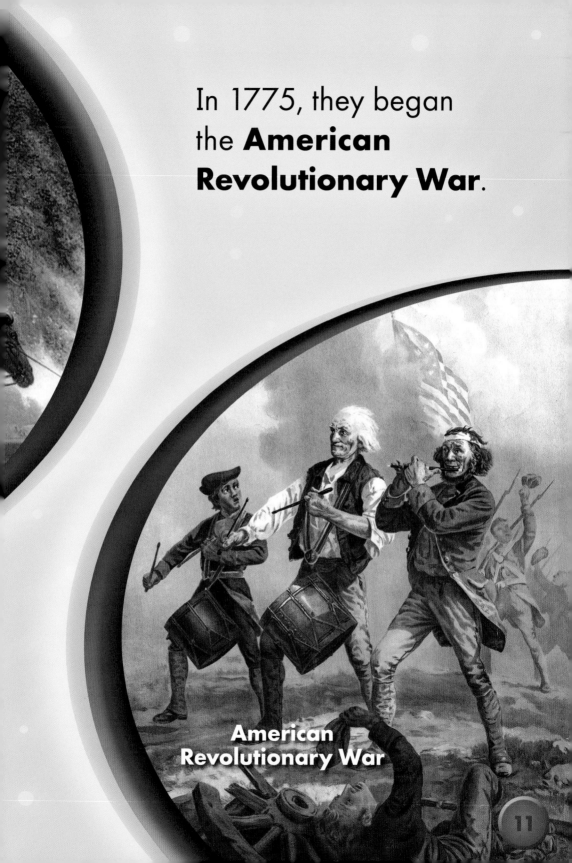

American Revolutionary War

American leaders agreed upon the **Declaration of Independence** on July 4, 1776.

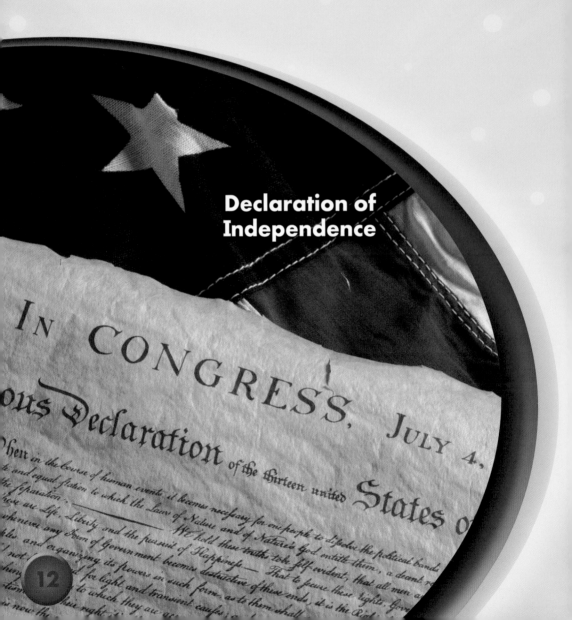

Declaration of Independence

American Independence Timeline

April 19, **1775**	American Revolutionary War begins
July 4, **1776**	Continental Congress approves the Declaration of Independence
September 3, **1783**	Treaty of Paris ends the American Revolutionary War
January 14, **1784**	The United States of America is officially formed

The American colonies won the war years later. The United States of America became a free country!

Time to Celebrate

The United States holds Independence Day on July 4. It became a national holiday in 1870.

Today, many people celebrate
with summer activities.

Independence Day Traditions!

People watch fireworks
at fairgrounds or parks.

Cities in every state shoot off booming displays! Some families buy sparklers to light at home.

sparkler

Many families and friends have barbecues. They grill hamburgers and hot dogs. Some eat corn on the cob and cake. Children play games or go to the beach.

Make Patriotic Pudding Pops

These sweet treats can keep you cool on a hot July day.

Recipe

What You Need:
- 3.4-ounce box instant vanilla pudding mix
- 2 cups cold milk
- large mixing bowl
- 3 small mixing bowls
- red and blue food coloring
- mixing spoon
- 4 paper drink cups
- 4 popsicle sticks
- bowl of warm water

What You Do:
1. In the large bowl, stir together pudding mix and milk.
2. Evenly divide the pudding between the three smaller bowls.
3. Add red food coloring to one bowl.
4. Add blue food coloring to a second bowl.
5. Spoon the red pudding into the bottom of the paper cups.
6. Next, spoon the white pudding over the red.
7. Then, top the white pudding with the blue.
8. Push a popsicle stick into the center of each cup.
9. Freeze the cups for several hours or until frozen.
10. Dip each cup into warm water for a few seconds. The paper cup will slide off. Enjoy!

Cities have Fourth of July parades. Marching bands play **patriotic** songs. **Military** troops carry American flags. Floats are decorated with stars and stripes.

Americans celebrate their freedom!

Glossary

American Revolutionary War—the American war for independence from Great Britain that lasted from 1775 to 1783; the Americans won the war and formed the United States of America.

colonies—lands owned and settled by people from another country

colonists—people who live in colonies

Declaration of Independence—a formal document that says the American colonies are free from British rule

military—the armed forces

national—related to the entire country

patriotic—showing love, honor, and respect for one's country

pinwheels—toys with fanlike blades that spin in the wind and are attached to a stick

To Learn More

AT THE LIBRARY

Appleby, Alex. *Happy Fourth of July!* New York, N.Y.: Gareth Stevens Publishing, 2014.

Landau, Elaine. *What Is the 4th of July?* Berkeley Heights, N.J.: Enslow Publishers, 2012.

Rissman, Rebecca. *Independence Day.* Chicago, Ill.: Heinemann Library, 2011.

ON THE WEB

Learning more about Independence Day is as easy as 1, 2, 3.

1. Go to www.factsurfer.com.

2. Enter "Independence Day" into the search box.

3. Click the "Surf" button and you will see a list of related web sites.

With factsurfer.com, finding more information is just a click away.

Index

The images in this book are reproduced through the courtesy of: ErickN, front cover (statue); laviana, front cover (flag); Daniel Dempster Photography/ Alamy, p. 4; Barbara Sauder, pp. 4-5; Monkey Business Images, pp. 6-7; wavebreakmedia, p. 7; Josef Hanus, p. 8; Ron_Thomas, pp. 8-9; Niday Picture Library/ Alamy, pp. 10-11; kreicher, p. 11; jcphoto, p. 12; Joe Sohm/ Alamy, p. 13 (circle stars); Sean Pavone/ Alamy, p. 14; M_a_y_a, pp. 14-15; Onest Mistic/ Getty Images, pp. 16-17; Ariel Skelley/ Getty Images, p. 17; Roger Tully/ Getty Images, p. 18; Lois Stanfield, p. 19 (all); ZUMA Press Inc/ Alamy, p. 20; MivPiv, p. 21; Susan Schmitz, p. 22 (hat).